T0198940

STOP
LEAVING
MONEY
ON THE TABLE

JASON M. FIELDS

author**HOUSE**®

AuthorHouse™
1663 Liberty Drive
Bloomington, IN 47403
www.authorhouse.com
Phone: 1 (800) 839-8640

Published by AuthorHouse 10/05/2018

ISBN: 978-1-5462-6328-9 (sc)
ISBN: 978-1-5462-6326-5 (hc)
ISBN: 978-1-5462-6327-2 (e)

Library of Congress Control Number: 2018911924

Print information available on the last page.

CONTENTS

SUMMARY:

This book is a compact guide about the need for financial planning and future investment in the African-American community within the United States. My aim is to provide information and advice about financial literacy, psychology and the important need to budget and invest for the future. African-Americans may be leaving their future down to chance if they do not fully understand the need for self-improvement in financial literacy. There should be an established financial education from an early age to help combat the poor choices that are often made because of this financial illiteracy. You cannot blame a community if the people were never offered any sound financial advice in the first place. Therefore my wish is to represent and inform African-Americans about the benefits of complete financial understanding.

INTRODUCTION:

In America today, the African-American community may be failing to realize the importance of financial planning and the psychology behind it. This is why all educational processes from a young age, such as high schools and through to college and universities should offer a comprehensive financial education curriculum that teaches the concepts of economics and the benefits of being financially aware in all aspects concerning personal and business finance. With the capability to apply proven techniques and logical financial strategies to help budget, invest and save, the future will be far brighter for African-Americans. This book intends to advize, inform and provide the community with sound financial advice and to hopefully offer support to those who wish to improve their financial literacy and become more financially aware for the future. I feel that the African-American community is currently underrepresented and this also includes mixed minorities, woman and veterans, etc. My intention and rationale is to look at this problem in depth and attempt to address it by assessing why communities of color need to be represented and offered more education about personal and business finances from an early age and into adulthood. We should never stop learning but unfortunately the underrepresented can have a hard time finding access to educational opportunities. This may lead to more difficulties in the future concerning access to capital and making sound financial decisions if they do improve their personal finances. Many times that is basically due to lack of exposure to personal, business and financial literacy and the important psychology that helps folk to prioritize their finances. I wish to educate and help people to break away from the past narrative because in essence, there is huge upsides for minorities when they can begin to make good financial choices. With that, it will also effect the community they live in positively and the entire country will benefit economically. That is why I decided to create this book. I want it to be a go-to resource for those who wish to be educated and enlightened about the long-term effects of understanding personal financial matters. Hopefully my work will be very informative to schools and organizations alike, and it can be read/ referenced to teach financial aspects and its concepts to children and adults from all walks of life, not just minority communities. Economics is the lifeblood of a country therefore learning the fundamental factors behind financial focus is a priority.

We should stop leaving money on the table and teach every community to understand the methodology of effective financial decision making.

1: THE NEED FOR LITERACY IN THE AFRICAN-AMERICAN COMMUNITY

Financial illiteracy can lead to under-achievement and economical deficiency. That is why there is such an important need in society for literacy to be at the forefront of education, especially in the African-American communities. A vast amount of income is passed through African-Americans hands on a yearly basis. However, this money can be put to better use if the people are more financially astute. Minority communities do struggle when it comes to implementing financial strategies. Simply because they may be illiterate about the benefits of the correct procedures concerning financial planning. Consequentially, without financial literacy being established and taught correctly to the community it will only end in financial failure amongst its peers. Financial literacy to a person is being able to possess the skills and knowledge that allows that individual to make informed and effective decisions with all of their financial resources. We, as a minority community must raise interest in personal and business finance to ensure our peers can prosper. We must understand the basic concepts before moving on to more advanced financial systems. It is a fact that people who have learned the appropriate literacy are then capable of making better financial decisions and they manage their finances much better than those who unfortunately have had no such training. It is my opinion that we should campaign for a for a financial literacy education that is more oriented and broader in focus. The African-American community should be offered a curriculum that helps each individual, no matter of their schooling, to better understand financial factors and the risks in not having sound financial judgement.

The Organization for Economic Co-operation and Development started an international governmental project with the initiative and objective of providing ways to improve financial education and literacy standards. But unfortunately many individuals within African-American communities are still not receiving this exposure to help educate them. This may be due to personal circumstances including their family life, school life or even gang life. Yet we must try to persist and educate the people until everyone is capable of financial prosperity. We must offer a wealth of information to the country as a whole and be confident that financial training is available to all.

Measures have been put in place to support further financial literacy education and many organizations have empowered the literacy movement. They may differ somewhat on their definitions of financial literacy but the President's Advisory Council on Financial Literacy has called for a consistent definition of financial literacy by which all financial education programs can be judged. It is now defined as 'the ability to use the knowledge and skills to successfully manage financial resources effectively for a lifetime of financial well-being'. However the Council for Economic Education in the United States found that out of 44 states that currently have K-12 personal finance education and its guidelines in place, only 17 states actually require high school students to enrol on a course in personal finance. This may be the reason why so many people are failing with their personal finances. Or maybe it is because students, especially in the minority communities are dependent upon the initiative of their local schooling board and its awareness to employ the proper financial learning facilities to the student.

The current approach therefore may be lacking in its ability to inform the students and the educators are performing their duties from a deficit perspective. Hence, the educator is seen as the expert providing the knowledge to a passive student who may not realize the true benefits of what is being taught. For that reason the student can lack interest. We must find a way to change this mentality and recommend an approach that would incorporate a transformative learning framework with its basic fundamentals as per the National Endowment for Financial Educations model. Which is the framework that is most established with adults who fully understand the benefits of financial education. Within that framework, students have embarked through the correct psycho-cultural process of acquiring new and revised interpretations of financial beliefs, attitudes and perspectives that help to shape their financial behavior. These kinds of alternative approaches can help individuals to examine and re-evaluate their current thoughts and mindset about personal finance. It helps to increase self-awareness and empowers people from all walks of life to establish the benefits of applying long-term positive money habits that can assure greater financial security and personal lifestyle stability. This is certainly so, and that is exactly what we should aim for within the African-American community.

Our aim for the economy should be to learn our diverse communities about the importance of financial literacy and the correct procedures concerned with the management of their personal finances. The procedures should be taught to colored youths as well as Caucasians from an early age such as in high school. Whether that be an expensive private school or a public school, financial education is a must. Because, all should know the true value of money management.

Financial literacy is key to creating and sustaining wealth for the African-American communities in the US. It is a legacy that must be passed down like an inheritance in the family. From an early age we should educate our children about financial literacy and the need to be financially literate in our economy. This will strengthen the African-American community and provide our peers with the possibilities and opportunity to create future wealth.

2: WHAT IS YOUR FINANCIAL PSYCHOLOGY?

This is the key question individuals must ask themselves because once that question is debated and finally answered, the person will then understand the reasons behind their spending habits and current financial circumstances. The majority of people who suffer with financial problems can be due to the result of their psychology. Factors including, where you were raised, what you were taught in childhood, family attitudes and subconscious beliefs towards spending and saving money can have a huge impact on your mindset and behavior.

The two biggest problems concerning financial issues in America are spending too much money and not saving enough for the future. However, in the minority communities this may slightly differ to include a very low-level of income and lower net worth due to lack of education, employment and bad financial behavior from an early age and into adulthood. Which has resulted in not enough funds in the first place to even contemplate saving for a rainy day and/or a higher crime rate in the community due to individuals trying to solve their money problems.

Should the minority blame the government for their financial difficulties?

Should they blame their childhood and their parents?

Or is it the individuals character and personality type that is to blame?

Well, the answer could be yes to both but the blame is substantially down to poor financial psychology. Therefore if the minority can be taught a different psychology from childhood to adulthood it will help to identify money management issues and how they relate to financial problems. This identification will lead to resolving financial matters in the person's favor.

The correct financial psychology procedures will address the issues associated with bad money management. Firstly, one must try to recognize the forces that influence the decision-making process, which can be down to past experiences, etc. Then, one must realize the psychological effects that are connected to loss or gain and the outcome the decision will have, either positively or negatively on your income. With that in place, you can be confident to make the correct decision to suit your needs. Nobody likes to experience loss therefore it is a no-brainer because you were able to apply the right psychological thought processes related to constructive financial management.

It is basically behavioral finance, which is the application of concepts and principles connected to the psychology of the understanding and management of money. How we think and feel about it will have a significant impact on our decisions concerning income. On an individual basis, personal misperceptions about finance and the correct psychology behind it, can have a detrimental effect and profound impact on the individuals life. Surprisingly, money management means different things to different people. To some, good money management means safety and survival. To others, money and the management behind it can mean superiority and power over peers because earning money and managing it better than others is how they rate their self-worth.

Understanding your financial psychology could be extremely beneficial as it can save you a lot of money. There are many different personality types that determine a person's financial psychology. And there are different psychological theories and economic surveys that further explain these types in more depth. However, I have chosen snippets from an article that I read some time ago in the *Financial Times* to help you to understand the basics and try to determine the fundamental aspects of the question, 'what is your financial psychology'?

- *Are you someone who always picks up the bill on a night out?* If so, your extreme generosity may not stem from huge wealth, but from status anxiety.

- *Do you always check your bank balance or investment portfolio?* You may feel like a spreadsheet specialist but in fact, you may be over-compensating for a lack of control elsewhere in your life.

- *Maybe you consider yourself as a budgeting champion because you know how to spot a bargain?* What if your drive to spend money on things that you don't really need and this could signify loneliness and/or a lack of self-esteem.

The above is a form of financial psychology at work. Factors like that can certainly be overlooked by a financially uneducated individual. But if the individual is offered this kind of education they will understand how they think and act can influence their financial environment. This knowledge will affect how they control their future finances.

Why?

Because the individual now has the superiority to control it instead of being controlled by their usual financial behavior. This will then turn the person to appreciate the importance of good money management and it may lead to rational investments, more savings and those impulsive spending sprees can become a thing of the past. Risky patterns like addictive buying or getting into debt will surely be eradicated if the person can recognize their financial psychology plays the most important part. Because of its underlying issues that trigger problem behavior.

So with that in mind, let us investigate some of the personality traits that psychologists and economists suggest are the most popular in financial psychology.

1. *The Anxious Investor;* although anxious, this personality trait is a lover of risks. They believe that they have an edge over others. Overconfidence can cloud their judgement leading to failure in markets. This kind of psychology is extremely common among affluent investors.

2. *The Hoarder;* money represents security for this personality trait. They avoid risks and tend to stockpile cash that they would be better off investing. If a person was raised in a family where money was extremely tight, they may have this type of personality that needs a lot of security and stability.

3. *The Social Spender;* shopping make this personality happy. Thee individual may frequently buy loved ones presents and blow their budget on occasions like

birthdays, etc. This type of frequent spending boosts self-esteem. But it is financial psychology that can cause addictive behavior leading to lack of personal funds. It is the same trait as the 'cash splasher'. They view themselves as generous but flashing the cash is usually to make people think more highly of them.

4. *The Financier;* Checking the bank balance and tracking all purchases and spending activity is this personality traits forte. It is a kind of financial psychology characteristic that can make an individual become obsessed with comparison sites, credit card points and switching providers to make them feel more in control of their finances, etc. It can be simply down to the desire to control, however this behavior's real trigger could be about anxiety in other parts of their life.

The above is just a short list of the personality traits considered in financial psychology. Albeit, financial psychology is a relatively new field of study, however there are many different personality traits considered by psychologists. All integrate psychology with financial management. It is a different way to look at financial and emotional well-being and to process the beliefs, emotions and behaviors related to money.

Applying the correct financial psychology can lead to more power, freedom and many other things. Therefore an individual must seek to understand their own financial psychology and implement techniques and strategies to help them to change direction if need be. This will positively affect their decision-making capabilities and lead to beneficial financial management in the future. The key to making better choices and decisions about money begins with understanding your own approach to spending, earning, saving and investing. Once that is understood, you can start to develop a positive style of financial management.

3: THE NEED TO BUDGET

The need to budget is of great importance, especially in the current turbulent economy. Budgeting money will help to create stability and security. It is a systematic approach that will help you to stay on top of your finances and pay the bills, etc. If an individual can manage their money effectively it will certainly contribute to their current lifestyle situation and future wealth and well-being. By understanding where and when money is coming in and where/when it is going out, it will enable a person to have full control over their personal and/or business finances. Good money management is essential to avoid and eradicate debt which may cause serious concerns to the person, like mental health issues and financial disaster. There are so many benefits from budgeting your money and by creating a spending plan it allows you to determine in advance whether you will have enough money to cover your needs and to do the things that you want to do. Budgeting is simply balancing your expenses with your income.

The most common types of budgeting include:

- Personal budget

- Master budget

- Operating budget

- Cash budget

- Static budget

- Flexible budget

- Capital expenditure budget

- Program budget

There are many reasons to why there is a need to budget and some include:

1. It ensures you don't spend money that you shouldn't.

2. It helps you to keep your eye on the target and end goal.

3. It can lead to a happy retirement.

4. It helps to prepare for unexpected emergencies.

5. It sheds light on spending habits.

6. It creates financial awareness.

Maintaining a budget on a regular basis will help you to keep track of personal/business expenses, analyze your income and anticipate all your present and future needs. The five main steps to preparing a budget are:

Step 1: Identify your goals

Step 2: Review what you have, i.e. income

Step 3: Define your costs

Step 4: Create the budget

Step 5: Keep track and stay on top

Creating a budget is a great tool that will help with decision making and this kind of good money management is a means to monitor personal and business performance. It will help to assess the current situation and to plan effectively to combat any financial difficulties helping towards a profitable outcome for the person or business at hand. Because if you are able to track how much money you have coming in and you know your recurring expenses, then you will find it much easier to live within your means.

Everybody should create a budget plan and monitor their finances.

Although you can live without a budget, if you do, it is like flying blind. Without a budget plan in place, it is difficult to assess what your financial situation really is. A budget provides an individual with the important information that is needed to make positive financial decisions.

The foundation of any budget plan is money coming in and money going out.

It helps you to determine your financial needs by calculating your income/expenses and figuring the difference between the two. Knowing that you can at least meet your monthly expenditure will give you peace of mind. If you realize a potential shortfall with your finances, you can consider ways to counteract it confidently. Basically, realizing and accepting the need to budget then creating a plan to manage your money will improve your overall cash flow. It is by far the best way to avoid cash flow problems. By reviewing your financial position on a monthly basis it will enable you to continue to pay the bills and hopefully to set some money aside for future purposes and to put to good use. A budget plan is a financial record and analysis of the money you earn and how you are spending that money. This record will become the basis for a plan to create improved spending habits. A monthly budget should focus on analysing and answering these questions:

- What amount is your total income?

- What percentage of your income are you spending on housing costs, food, transport, clothing, etc?

- What percentage is spent on essentials and what is spent on impulse buying?

- What is your level of debt?

- How will you cover that debt from your income?

- How much money are you saving?

- How does your spending habits represent your lifestyle priorities?

- Will you reach your monthly objectives?

- Are you in profit or loss at the end of each budget plan?

Creating a plan with those questions in mind and that assesses your spending patterns will benefit the most because you can then apply the methods to enable change if your balance is always in the red at the end of each month.

Budgeting is the art of analyzing and improving your spending habits. It is very much a balancing act. You must balance consistency with flexibility, self-discipline with realism and a sense of control with the occasional self-indulgence. The need to budget is obvious….

If you are wise and you care about your finances......You will understand the need to budget.

4: ARE YOU SAVING?

A survey in the US found that four out of ten American workers are not currently saving for their retirement. If workers are not implementing saving strategies then surely statistics will be much worse with the unemployed and within the minority communities that may struggle to make good financial decisions. Learning to save is the first step to guaranteeing a better future. However the problem many people have with saving is that it is the last thing they think of doing or even want to do with their hard-earned money. Most spend their money mentally before they even receive it. This can cause a mindset that will not even contemplate saving because the person thinks he/she cannot save. This mindset will eventually lead to financial difficulties in the future and it leads us to the question....

Why do so many people believe they cannot save?

Maybe it is because some think that the basic daily cost of living does not afford them any money left over to save for a rainy day. Or maybe the real reason is that they have never had any financial advice about saving and the strategies to help them to implement saving techniques for the future. I believe it is the latter. If people had the knowledge about how to save and how to do it effectively, they will continue to learn and progress with the actual experience of saving. That is why financial education must be available in abundance to minority communities in the US.

It may be true that the minority like African-Americans consistently underperform when it involves statistics on saving. This can be due to a complicated web of logistical and cultural factors. It is not simply down to poor personal choices and money decisions made throughout the community. It can also be due to the fact that a very high percentage of America's financial advisors are Caucasian leading to a lack of racial diversity within the financial industry. This can make it more difficult for professionals to actively educate and engage with minority communities. Therefore we must try to eradicate this lack of engagement and correct the communication to increase the African-American communities awareness about their personal finances and how to start applying saving strategies. We should increase financial literacy by providing greater access to simple and automated products and saving services. We should continue to support an increased diversity in the financial trade and amongst its financial advisors. This will help to affect communication positively as it will take socioeconomic and cultural factors including diversity and language barriers into account.

African-Americans must be educated about the first step to building personal wealth which is implementing saving strategies. Saving is putting money into a virtually risk-free financial vehicle, where it can safely grow over time. Saving should have a significant place in African-Americans personal financial plans. Their first financial goal should be to create and build up savings to help protect themselves in case of an emergency in the future. Many minority communities have not had that education about the benefits of saving.

Saving money is advantageous because it provides people the opportunity to earn interest while keeping their money safe. This is one of the great habits of wealthy people. The rich get richer because of the way they spend and save their money. Applying saving strategies will enable an individual to create successful habits of controlling their expenses and using the left-over income in order to grow their wealth. Although interest rates on savings accounts can be low at first, they still provide a profit that continues to rise the longer the money is being saved. Once an adequate emergency saving fund is established it can provide the seed money for higher yielding investments such as stocks, bonds and mutual funds. We will cover that in the next chapter but saving is the first important step for African-Americans to take before further consideration.

At least 20% of personal income should go towards saving. Meanwhile, another 50% should go towards necessities, while 30% can go towards discretionary items. This is called the 50/30/20 rule and it is a great rule for African-Americans to follow because it will provide them with the opportunity to save while they fund their everyday living costs.

Opening a savings account is easy and it will provide these instant benefits:

- Instant interest rates that provide an opportunity to earn money on your money.

- Growth of savings without added monthly fees.

- Easy access to your money.

- Automatic deposit set-up to help build on your savings.

- Free to open.

The income rankings in the US have remained unchanged for three decades amongst Caucasians, Asians, Hispanics and African-Americans. this can be due to folk not saving for the future. That is why we must educate our communities about saving and investing to secure a more prosperous economical future for America and its residents. Several years from now it is thought that Caucasian households are projected to own 86 times more wealth than the ordinary African-American households. We must change that statistic by educating the minority about applying saving strategies to change their spending habits and to grow their income. If we do nothing, then there will continue to be an income level gap and it will likely experience a downward slide in African-American wealth. One report that was recently created suggested by indicating evidence that by the year 2020, African-American households may stand to lose nearly 18% of their current wealth. While Caucasian households are expected to rise by 3%. Researchers say that this spells major economic peril for our nation. If this racial divide of finances continues to accelerate, the economic conditions of African-American households will have an adverse impact on the economy because the minority will increase to a majority that will no longer hold enough wealth to stake their claim in the middle-class. The tax system in America does not help the situation because it currently helps the wealthy households get wealthier. While African-Americans who are making 'middle-income-money' are at serious risk of becoming poorer. This is suggested that it is because African-Americans started off generations behind the richer Caucasian society and then encountered the red tape formalities and racially restrictive housing covenants of the early-to-middle 20th century. This prevented the sale of housing to the African-American community and isolated them together in much poorer communities in the US that subsequently lost value as Caucasians fled to the wealthier suburbs. Recent economic crises have only widened the wealth gap as the minority communities obviously took the impact of that economic hit. Therefore the wealth of African-Americans has never fully recovered. But surely it is time for that wealth gap to experience change.

If we can implement the change in our communities it would mean financial stability with the possible rise in funds to help African-Americans weather challenging economic storms. Also, it will enable the people to save some of their money and to invest in economic opportunities for their future children of America. Then the country as a whole may start to invest more in the minority than it has done in past situations. So, for that reason we should teach all African-Americans about the need to save and grow their personal wealth.

We need to educate African-American communities why it pays to save. If people save regularly they will find that their savings quickly increase and keep growing. Teaching good habits related to saving will enable them to watch their money turn into more money. The easiest way to start saving and to make it work for the individual is to set things up so that they automatically add income from their earnings by putting a little aside each month like we have already discussed. Then they can sit back and watch their wealth increase monthly. Simply setting up a 'standing order' via a current account to their savings account can generate a route to wealth. The best saving plan to implement is one where you can put money in on a pay day. Putting money aside just after you have been paid and before you start spending is the best way to save successfully. This will help to create a habit of saving regularly and that habit is important because with it in place, you will be very surprised at how quickly even a few dollars each payday tends to build up. As the money does build up, it will grow even faster because of higher interest rates, etc. This is because each time the interest earned on your money that it is paid into the savings account, it will start earning interest too. The interest-on-interest is called compound interest and over the longer term it can make a large difference to how much your personal savings are worth.

An individual must first work out how much they can viably save on a monthly basis, which is usually best. Then they can put that money aside without any financial risk to their current lifestyle. With savings started they can then stop leaving their money on the table and look forward to a brighter financial future.

5: WHY AFRICAN-AMERICANS MUST INVEST

Investing involves committing money into an investment vehicle in the hope of making financial gain. Investing is different from saving because it involves a greater level of risk. There is also no guarantee that you will get your money back on an investment. However, investing is known to have great rewards too. With a little set aside each payday or from a person's savings account it is very easy to invest and become a profitable investor if you can understand the stock market and its basic fundamentality's. You can even make regular payments into investment products such as stocks and shares, trusts and popular investment funds that will enable the opportunity to make a quick return on the dollar. The benefits related to investing are substantial if you can get it right. And for that reason, I strongly believe that African-Americans must invest to help secure their future.

Investment products can provide a quick cash injection but they are normally for the long term and generally suitable if you already have enough savings to keep you going for at least 3-6 months. Investments outperform cash savings over the longer term too, but their value can fluctuate by rising or falling. So a person must be prepared to take some risk. However, investing definitely deserves a place in an African-American's personal financial plan. Once they have accumulated an emergency cash savings fund and they are ready to consider investing, the investor will find that there are many options available for obtainable investments. Some are:

- *Shares;* a share is a security that represents part-ownership in a company. When a person buys a 'share', they are purchasing a small part of the business. This enables them to be entitled to a portion of the company profits. Investing in shares make you a viable shareholder entitled to the annual dividends.

- *Bonds;* a bond is basically an IOU. When you buy a bond, you are actually lending money to a company or a governmental agency/organization, etc. The institution that issues the bond will promise to pay you back with a fixed amount of interest at regular intervals over a set period of time. (The term). It will also repay the amount borrowed. (The principal). On a fixed date agreed by all concerned. This is also known as (the maturity date) of the bond in question.

- *Unit trusts;* a unit trust is a portfolio of securities (which are shares and/or bonds) created by an investment company or other registered financial service. When you invest in a unit bond you are buying into that company's portfolio and you will be offered your share in the dividends of interest as well as the increase or decrease in value of the collective investment.

- *Exchange traded products;* this is a type of pooled investment that is traded on the stock exchange like ordinary shares. This is a very popular type of security that is rapidly gaining ground. It offers many of the features of a unit trust and each share that is owned buy the trader represents a part ownership of the underlying portfolio and its returns. ETPs can be bought and sold throughout the trading day.

The obtainable list of particular investment vehicles is quite large which is great for the trading business in general. Investors from all walks of life can make their fortune by investing in vehicles that offer high returns on their investments. However, African-Americans are at a much higher risk for not meeting their personal investment goals. This is because some may think that investing has become more difficult across their community. Due to their current circumstances concerning financial awareness and that their basic money management capabilities are at a loss due to poorer education about constructive financial matters.

Those who are not investing have stated in a recent financial survey that represented the minority, that they don't invest because they actually don't have enough money to do so, (40%). And the survey further states that some people simply don't know how to invest, (34%). And (13%) are completely overburdened by student loans. The other (13%) held no opinion.

That financial survey alone, tells us that we must develop more opportunity for the people of our communities to invest, and we should provide as much information about the benefits of investing in products and services and how it will help to secure their financial future. There is information to be found at present but we must try to provide substantially more. 'Dvdendo' has developed an automated investment platform that is actually aimed at the minority. It is designed to improve investment awareness, foster education and boost investment access. Albeit, it is available to any US citizen but African-Americans in particular should research and use this tool which allows you to place funds in a brokerage account and invest in a portfolio of securities if your choice. This tool has great features that will certainly benefit the African-American who is wanting to invest for their future. The features include:

- No credit check

- Unlimited deposits and withdrawals

- No minimum investment amount

- $1 monthly fee for balances $5,000 or less; 0.25% annual advisory fee for balances over $5,000

- Debit or credit card linking for additional savings when you spend

- Social connection options for sharing progress with family and friends

This type of approach in using technology as an awareness mechanism for consumers including the minority communities is now recognized by financial professionals as the much-needed push to help people to do more with their money and secure their financial futures by provoking an investment mentality. The benefits are certainly there for all to see, the features offered very good indeed. Therefore it is my opinion that all African-Americans should at least consider jumping on the investing bandwagon and try to make money on their hard-earned money.

There are many market sectors available to an investor and some are:

- Mobile telecommunications

- Electronic and electrical equipment

- Pharmaceuticals and biotechnology

- Construction and metals

- Technology hardware and software equipment

- Mining

- Oil and gas production

- Personal goods

- Life insurance

- Aerospace and defence

- Gas, water and multi-utilities

- Food and drug retailers

- Overseas investments

- And many more

Most investors agree that the best place for most people to start investing is with unit trusts, OEIC or broad market ETF. After the investor has gained that experience they may choose to graduate investing directly in shares. Smart share investing is considered the best way to amass significant wealth. Whatever choice is made, you should always do your homework so that you choose your investment vehicles and specific investments wisely. Investing for the future will certainly serve an individual in their retirement. African-Americans should choose an investment plan that fits their budget. You really don't need substantial wealth to start investing. But the right plan for you depends on your personal circumstances. You can ask yourself these following questions to help guide your investment decisions:

1. How much can you invest? By assessing your living needs it will determine how much you can afford to set aside for investments.

2. How much do you want or need to earn on your investments, what type of payback do you need or expect from the money invested?

3. How long do you plan to invest?

4. What is your level of risk tolerance? Some investments are more certain than others. These investments that are more secure pay lower rates of return than higher risks.

A variety of financial professionals can guide and help you to identify all of your investment questions and available options. But you are the only person who knows what your goals are and you are responsible for your own finances. Therefore do be aware of the risks associated with the investments you choose to make. Asking for professional advice can be the best way to assure investment success.

The recent proliferation of stock and bond variations, individual retirement accounts, and an assortment of other investment opportunities make finding the right investments a tough proposition so before you invest your money, you should do some research by reading up on investments, browsing the internet, talking to other investors and to contact investment professionals. By turning to someone who is professionally trained and certified it will help you to find sound financial advice and investment counsel. A certified financial planner will have completed the educational requirements that is needed by passing an exam administered by the Certified Financial Planning Board od Standards. You could also seek help from an accredited personal finance specialist who has been accredited as a financial planner by the American Institute of Certified Public Accountants. In a situation that is as personal and important as your finances, you want someone you can trust and feel completely comfortable with. Look at the hard facts, such as their credentials and financial experience before taking them on as an advizor.

The beneficial factors from investments are plenty. Investments let your money work for you. In addition to contributing to your retirement fund, investments can help you in many other ways such as the following:

- Earning an income on excess cash can be a great way to increasing your personal finances.

- It makes your money work for you by earning that much wanted interest and profits.

- By setting aside a portion of your income in certain investments, you can put off paying taxes for a short time. Investment income is often called deferred income because it gets taxed at a later date.

- Investing will contribute to a more comfortable retirement.

To be eligible for some of these benefits, you must take advantage of investments that are prescribed by the IRS. Investments that offer tax incentives are as follows:

1. Tax-free money market funds

2. Tax-free stock or bond mutual funds

3. Municipal bonds

4. Treasury bonds

5. Retirement accounts such as IRA's, SEP-IRA's and SIMPLE plans.

African-Americans can find a variety of ways to invest their money, some that give specific considerations to the minority like we have already covered. The most important thing to remember about investing is to keep your expectations reasonable. The chances of getting rick and doing it quickly are slim but people who study the markets diligently can earn high returns. Therefore I again suggest that African-Americans should stop leaving their money on the table and let it start to earn an additional income for them to believe and achieve in their future.

ABOUT THE AUTHOR:

J M. Fields is a financial professional who is the founder of the company www.thefinancialpromise.com

He is dedicated to educating and helping people to change their personal financial circumstances for the better. The Financial Promise's mission is to be dedicated in working with communities to increase personal financial and business literacy so that they can invest in themselves to build financial stability, develop their careers and to create their own businesses to help increase their personal wealth. The company vision is to be recognized as a trusted leader that helps community members improve their chances of success by making smarter financial decisions. It is a company that offers a lot to people from all walks of life including from minority backgrounds who have not had the opportunity tom seek personal advancement in the financial world.

The Financial promise's Personal Finance and Business Literacy curriculum and presentations on offer are engaging and fun, yet they also meet core educational standards. The programming has been widely recognized for its ability to connect with students, managers, and CEO's and it inspires all participants of all ages and socioeconomic backgrounds to take positive financial action.

Consumers must confront complicated financial decisions at a very young age in today's demanding financial environment, and financial mistakes made early in life can be extremely costly. Therefore young people often find themselves carrying large amounts of student loans or credit card debt, and such early entanglements can hinder their ability to accumulate wealth. The financial promise helps young adults to make decisions that will limit any further financial mistakes in the future.

The company's dynamic financial literacy curriculum for 9-12th graders in the US, features an engaging design, student-centered activities, research projects, discussion points, and tools and resources that are all-designed to engage students in learning the personal finance skills that they need to succeed in life after high school.

INVESTING DEFINITIONS

Unsure about a term? Check out our Glossary. From Asset Allocation to Zero-coupon bonds, we'll help you catch the buzz in no time.

A ...

ADV form - Form on file with the Securities and Exchange Commission that contains important financial information about a registered investment advisor.

Advisor (Adviser) - 1. Person or company responsible for making mutual fund investments. 2. Organization employed by a mutual fund to give professional advice on the fund's investments and asset management practices. Also known as investment advisor.

Aggressive growth funds - Mutual funds that strive for maximum growth as the primary objective.

Annual report - Updates that detail performance for the year.

Annual return - The percentage of change in a mutual fund's net asset value over a year's time, factoring in income dividend payments, capital gains, and reinvestment of these distributions.

Asset-allocation fund - Balanced fund in which changes are made in the stock and bond percentage mix, based on the outlook for each market.

Automatic investment plan - Program that allows you to have as little as $50 a month electronically deducted from your checking account and invested in the mutual fund of your choice.

Average price per share - Most popular method of paying taxes on mutual fund sales, in which you calculate gains or losses by first figuring an average cost per share. You calculate the total cost of all the fund shares you own and divide that by the number of shares you own.

B ...

Balanced funds - Mutual funds that invest in both stocks and bonds, typically in relatively equal proportions.

Bear market - Period during which the stock market loses more than 10 percent of its value.

Beta value - Measure of a fund's volatility. The lower the beta value, the less risky the fund.

Blue-chip stocks - Stocks issued by well-established companies that pay dividends.

Bond - A debt instrument issued by a company, city, or state, or the U.S. government or its agencies, with a promise to pay regular interest and return the principal on a specified date.

Bull market - Period during which the stock market moves higher for a couple of years straight.

C ...

Callable - Debt that may be redeemed before it matures.

Capital appreciation funds - Mutual funds that strive for maximum growth. Although these funds can earn the greatest gains, they also can rack up the heaviest losses. Also known as aggressive growth funds.

Capital gains - Profits on the sale of securities.

Certificates of Deposit (CD's) - Debt instruments issued by banks and thrifts.

Certified Financial Planner (CFP) - Financial planner that has been awarded his or her certification by the International Board of Standards for Certified Financial Planners. To become CFP licensees, candidates must first demonstrate they have completed a personal financial planning curriculum, then pass a 10-hour board examination that tests their knowledge of the components of financial planning. In addition, all CFP licensees must fulfill a continuing education requirement and abide by the CFP Board's Code of Ethics and Professional Responsibility.

Charitable lead trust - Legal document used to avoid estate taxes, in which the charity receives the investment income and the principal goes to the trust beneficiaries when you die.

Charitable remainder trust - Legal document set up with a charity, in which the charity pays you income for life. When you die, the money goes to the charity, tax-free.

Check-a-month plan - Program through which money is automatically taken out of your checking account and invested in your mutual fund.

Closed-end funds - Funds whose shares are traded on an exchange, similar to stocks. The price per share doesn't typically equal the net asset value of a share.

Common stock - Unit of ownership in a public corporation with voting rights, but with lower priority than either preferred stock or bonds if the company is ever liquidated.

Constant dollar investing - Investment strategy that preserves profits by periodic evaluation and adjustment of a portfolio. You maintain the same amount in your stock fund each year by channeling funds from and to a bond or money market fund.

Convertible bond funds - Mutual funds that invest in bonds that can be converted into stocks.

Corporate bonds - Debt instruments issued by corporations.

Custodian - Bank or other financial institution that safeguards mutual fund securities and may respond to transactions only by designated fund officers.

D ...

Distributions - Dividends income and capital gains generally paid by mutual fund companies to their shareholders.

Diversification - Act of investing in different kinds of investments to lessen risk.

Diversified - Spread out, as among a variety of investments that perform differently.

Dividends - Profits that a corporation or mutual fund distributes to shareholders.

Dollar cost averaging - Strategy of making regular investments into a mutual fund and having earnings automatically reinvested. This way, when the share price drops, more shares are bought at lower prices.

Dow Jones Industrial Average - Model for the overall stock market that tracks the performance of 30 U.S. blue-chip stocks.

Duration - A way to measure part of the risk in a bond or bond fund. Duration tells you, in years, how long it will take you to recoup your principal investment. It makes for a handy way to judge the interest rate risk of your investment. *Example:* if a bond or abond fund has a duration of seven years (stated as 7.0), a 1% drop in interest rates will raise its value by 7%, while a 1% rise in interest rates will lower its price by 7%.

E ...

Equities - Investments in stocks and other assets.

Equity income funds - Mutual funds that favor investments in stocks that generate income over growth. As a result, they can be less risky than other types of stock funds.

Ex-dividend date - Date on which the value of the income or capital gains distribution is deducted from the price of a fund's shares.

F ...

Face value - Value of a bond or note as given on the certificate. Corporate bonds are usually issued with $1,000 face values, municipal bonds with $5,000 face values, and government bonds, $1,000 to $10,000 face values. Also known as the principal.

Financial planner - Individual who helps establish a financial game plan. Although a financial planner may have certain licenses or designations indicating the extent of his or her training, there is no requirement that a financial planner have a license. Financial planners carry professional designations, such as CFP and ChFC.

First In-First Out (FIFO) - Basis for calculating the tax impact of mutual fund profits and losses that assumes shares sold are the oldest shares owned.

Fixed-income fund - Another term for a mutual bond fund.

Front-end loads - Sales commission paid to purchase shares of mutual funds.

G ...

General purpose money funds - Mutual funds that invest largely in bank CDs and short-term corporation I.O.U.'s called commercial paper.

Global funds - Mutual funds that invest in both the U.S. and foreign countries. Also known as world funds.

Growth funds - Mutual funds that invest in the stocks of well-established firms that are expected to be profitable and grow for years to come.

Growth and income funds - Mutual funds that own primarily blue-chip stocks of well-established companies that pay out a lot of dividends to their shareholders. These funds generally develop stock portfolios that balance the potential for appreciation with the potential for dividend income.

H ...

Hedging - Strategy of investing in one or more securities to protect yourself from potential losses in other investments.

High-quality corporate bond funds - Mutual funds that buy bonds issued by the nation's financially strongest companies.

High-yield bond funds - Risky bond mutual funds that invest in high-yield bonds of companies with poor credit ratings. The bonds are rated below triple B by Standard ST Poor's and Moody's. Also known as junk bond funds.

I ...

Income - Periodic interest or dividend distributions obtained from a fund.

Income funds - Mutual funds that invest in higher-yielding stocks, but may own some bonds. You get income first along with some growth. These funds usually invest in utility, telephone and blue-chip stocks.

Inflation - Rise in prices of goods and services.

Inflation hedge - Term describing an investment that performs well when inflation heats up.

Insurance agent - Individual licensed to sell insurance.

Insured municipal bond funds - Mutual funds that invest in insured bonds issued by cities, towns, states, toll roads, schools, water projects, and hospitals. The interest income is tax-free, and the bonds are insured against default by large private insurance companies, such as American Municipal Pond Assurance Corp. (AMRAC) and Municipal Bond Insurance Association (MBIA).

Interest income - Earnings received, often from bonds.

Interest rate risk - This is the danger that prevailing interest rates will rise significantly higher than the rate paid on bonds or bond funds you are holding. This drives down the price of your bonds, so if you sell you'll lose money. This is a serious risk for anyone investing in long-term bonds, including Treasurys, because the longer the maturity, the higher the interest rate risk (see duration).

Intermediate-term bond funds - Mutual funds that invest in bonds that mature in about 5 to 10 years. International bonds Debt instruments issued by foreign governments or corporations.

International funds - Mutual funds that invest in stocks or bonds of worldwide companies.

Investment banker - Firm that sells stocks or bonds to brokerages which, in turn, sell them to investors on a securities exchange.

Investment company - Firm that, for a management fee, invests pooled funds of small investors in securities appropriate for its stated investment objectives.

Investment objective - Description, included in a fund prospectus, of what a mutual fund hopes to accomplish.

Irrevocable trust - Legal document that allows you to avoid probate and reduce the tax bite. You give up ownership of any asset you placed in this type of trust, and it can't be changed.

J ...

Junk bond funds - Mutual funds that invest in bonds issued by companies or governments that are rated below BBB by Standard and Poor's or Moody's. Also known as high-yield bond funds.

K ...

L ...

Long-term bond funds - Mutual funds that invest in bonds that mature in more than 10 years.

M ...

Management fee - Charge for running the fund.

Market timing - Strategy by which investors attempt to buy low and sell high by buying when the market is turning bearish and selling at the end of a bull market.

Maturity date - Date that a bond is due for payoff.

Money market mutual fund - Mutual fund that invests typically in short-term government and company loans and CDs. These tend to be lower-yielding, but less risky than most other types of funds. Also known as money market funds or money funds.

Municipal bond funds - Mutual funds that invest in tax-exempt bonds is sued by states and local governments.

N ...

Net asset value - Per-share value of your fund's investments. Also known as share price.

No-load mutual fund - Mutual fund that is sold without sales commission.

Note - Another word for short-term bond.

No-transaction fee account - Brokerage firm account that allows customers to purchase a selection of mutual funds with no charge or a limited charge.

O ...

Open-end funds - Funds that permit ongoing purchase and redemption of fund shares (mutual funds are open-end funds).

Over-the-counter market - Market that uses a network of brokers to buy and sell securities rather than an exchange.

P ...

Portfolio manager - Person responsible for making mutual fund investments.

Precious metals mutual fund - Mutual funds that invest in precious metals and mining stocks.

Preferred stock - Type of stock that takes priority over common stock in the payment of dividends or if the company is liquidated.

Principal - Original investment.

Prospectus - Legal disclosure document that spells out information you need to know to make an investment decision on a mutual fund or other security.

Q ...

R ...

Rebalancing - Investment strategy in which you adjust your mix of investments periodically to keep the proper percentages of money in each fund, based on your tolerance for risk.

Regional funds - Mutual funds that invest in one specific region of the globe.

Registered representative - Person licensed to sell stocks, bonds, mutual funds, and other types of securities.

Risk - In relation to a mutual fund, chances of losing money.

Risk tolerance - Amount of money you can stomach losing in a given year.

S ...

SAP 500 index - Measure of the performance of a large group of blue-chip stocks in the U.S.

Salary reduction plan or 401 (k) plan - Retirement plan that allows employees to have a percentage of their salaries withheld and invested prior to the payment of federal taxes. Often, the employer might match the contribution, and earnings are tax-deferred until retirement.

Secondary market - Market wherein bonds, stocks, or other securities are bought and sold after they're already issued.

Securities - Stocks, bonds, or rights to ownership, such as options, typically sold by a broker.

Securities exchange - Tightly regulated marketplace where stocks, bonds, and cash are traded.

Securities and Exchange Commission (SEC) - U.S. government agency in charge of regulating mutual funds and other securities.

Share - Unit of ownership.

Shareholder - One who owns shares. In a mutual fund, this person has voting rights.

Short-term bond funds - Mutual funds that generally invest in bonds that mature in less than three years.

Sectors - in financial circles, refers to a particular industry within a total economy, i.e. the 'oil sector' refers to those companies engaged in businesses relating to oil exploration, production, refining, pipelines, drilling, etc.

Simplified Employee Pension Plan (SEP) - Retirement plan that permits tax-deferred investments for self-employed individuals.

Single-country funds - Mutual funds or closed-end funds that invest in one country.

Single-state municipal bond funds - Mutual funds that invest in the bonds of a single state so that investors avoid paying both state and federal taxes on their interest income.

Small company stock funds - Volatile mutual funds that invest in younger companies whose stocks are frequently traded on the over-the-counter stock market.

Socially responsible funds - Mutual funds that invest in companies that do not pollute the environment or sell arms. They will not own tobacco or alcohol stocks, nor invest in companies with poor employee relations.

Specialty funds - Funds that invest in one specific industry or industry sector.

Speculation - Gambling on a risky investment in hopes of a high payoff down the road.

Spreads - For bonds, a spread is a difference in prices of similar bonds that vary in only one point, such as the quality. For options, a spread is a combination of two or more calls (or puts) on the same stock with differing exercise prices or times to maturity. For futures, a spread position is where the investor takes a long position in a futures contract of one maturity and a short position in a contract on the same commodity with a different maturity.

Stock - Investment that buys ownership in a corporation, in exchange for a portion of that company's earnings and assets.

Stockbroker - Person licensed to sell stocks and other types of securities. Also known as a registered representative.

Stock fund builder - Investment strategy in which you invest your bond fund's interest income into a stock fund to build your wealth.

Swap - Switch, as in what bond fund managers do to obtain higher-yielding bonds that have credit ratings similar or equal to their existing bonds.

T ...

Taxable bond funds - Bond mutual fund in which interest income is taxed by Uncle Sam.

Tax-deferred investment - An investment that is not taxed until money is withdrawn, usually at retirement.

Tax-free bond funds - Tax-free mutual funds that invest in municipal bonds issued by states, cities, and towns.

Testamentary trust - Legal document set up by a will when a person dies that is used for special situations, such as to establish a fund to pay for a child's education.

Total return - The rate of return on an investment, including reinvestment of distributions.

Transfer agent - Entity that maintains shareholder records, including purchases, sales, and account balances.

Treasury bills - Short-term I.O.U.'s to the U.S. Treasury.

Living Trust - A legal document that does not have to be approved by probate court before your loved ones can inherit your wealth.

12b-1 fee - Fee deducted from the earning of your mutual fund to cover a fund's sales and marketing expenses.

U ...

Uniform Gift to Minors Act (UGMA) - Law adopted in most states that sets rules for distribution of an investment to a child.

Uniform Transfer to Minors Act (UTMA) - Law in some states that governs how a child takes custody of an asset.

Uninsured high-yield municipal bond funds - Mutual funds that pay the highest tax-free yields but invest in states or municipalities with lower credit ratings.

U.S. government agency bonds - Debt instruments issued by federally sponsored agencies of the U.S. government.

U.S. Treasury bond funds - Mutual funds that invest in U.S. Treasury bonds and notes.

U.S. Treasury bonds - Debt instruments directly backed by the U.S. Treasury.

U.S. Treasury-only money funds - Funds that invest in Treasury bills, or T-bills, which are short-term I.O.U.'s to the U.S. Treasury. These funds typically pay the lowest yields but are considered the least risky money funds.

U.S. Treasury securities - Generally, Treasury notes, bills, or bonds issued and guaranteed by the U.S. government.

V ...

Variable annuities - An insurance program that allows you to direct your investment in a choice of underlying investments. Meanwhile, you get tax deferment of your earnings and a death benefit guarantee, and you are able to obtain periodic checks for life.

W ...

Wash sale - Strategy in which a security is bought back within 31 days after it is sold, 'washing out' any capability of writing off losses on income taxes.

World funds - Mutual funds that invest in both the U.S. and foreign countries. Also known as global funds.

X ...

Y ...

Yield - Interest or market earnings on a bond or other investment.

Yield Curve - A graph of the bond yields available at a given moment in time, with yield-to-maturity rising along the vertical line and bond maturities moving outward along the horizontal line. A normal yield curve rises upward to the right, because bonds of a longer maturity generally pay higher yields. An inverted yield curve slopes downward to the right because short-term rates are higher than long-term rates. There may be several reasons for an inverted yield curve such as higher anticipated inflation in the short run versus the long run or possibly a recession in the offing. If short and long-term rates are the same, the yield curve is flat. The yield curve is typically constructed using Treasury securities.

Z ...

Zero coupon Treasury bond funds - Mutual funds that invest in a certain type of Treasury securities that provide no monthly income, but, instead, pay the investor accumulated income and principal at the bond's maturity.

Printed in the United States
By Bookmasters